FIGHTER PLANES

PHYLLIS EMERT

JULIAN  MESSNER

WILD WINGS

For Josh and Beth Berner

The author wishes to acknowledge the Carruthers Aviation Collection, Sprague Library, Harvey Mudd College, Claremont, California, and express thanks to Nancy R. Waldman, Librarian, Sprague Library, for her help and cooperation in preparation of the *Wild Wings* series.

JULIAN MESSNER and colophon are trademarks of Simon & Schuster, Inc.
Manufactured in the United States of America.

Lib. ed. 10 9 8 7 6 5 4 3 2 1
Paper ed. 10 9 8 7 6 5 4 3 2 1

Library of Congress Cataloging-in-Publication Data

Emert, Phyllis Raybin.
　　Fighter planes / Phyllis Emert.
　　　　p.　cm. — (Wild wings)
　　Includes bibliographical references.
　　Summary: Describes the specifications and uses of various fighter planes, including the Sopwith Camel, Messerchmitt ME 262-A Sturmvogel, and Lockheed F-104 Starfighter.
　　　1. Fighter planes—Juvenile literature.　[1. Fighter planes.
　2. Airplanes.]　　I. Title.　II. Series: Emert, Phyllis Raybin.　Wild wings.
UG1242.F5E44　　1990
358.4'3—dc20
　　　ISBN 0-671-68959-2 (lib. bdg.)　　ISBN 0-671-68964-9 (pbk.)
　　　　　　　　　　　　　　　　　　　　90-31489
　　　　　　　　　　　　　　　　　　　　CIP
　　　　　　　　　　　　　　　　　　　　AC

Photo credits and acknowledgments

Pages 14 and 17 courtesy of Grumman
Pages 22, 25, 46, and 49 courtesy of Experimental Aircraft
Pages 30 and 33 courtesy of U.S. Airforce Museum
Pages 18, 21, 34, 42, and 45 courtesy of Lockheed
Pages 26, 29, and 38 courtesy of North American Rockwell
Pages 50 and 53 courtesy of McDonnell Douglas
Pages 58 and 61 courtesy of General Dynamics

CONTENTS

INTRODUCTION

The main goal of a fighter plane is to fight. It provides a way of taking weapons into the air. The fighter's purpose is to destroy all enemy aircraft and make the airspaces safe.

Success as a fighter pilot is measured by how well the pilot uses his guns. The most successful fighter pilots were aggressive, self-confident, and dedicated to flying. These flying "aces" had little fear of being killed in battle.

Fighter planes serve in other important roles. Reconnaissance aircraft fly over enemy areas and gather information. Pilots note troop movements and placement of artillery. They also record the location of industries, population centers, railroad lines, highways, and other ground features and formations.

Information gathered by reconnaissance aircraft helps determine the tactics of warfare. Tactics are the way military forces are arranged and moved around in combat with the enemy.

Low-flying fighter planes are also used in ground assaults. They attack troops or positions with machine-gun fire, bombs, rockets, or missiles.

Fighter planes also act as escorts and fly along with heavy bombers or other aircraft. Their job is to protect them from the enemy.

Combat airplanes have become more complicated since they were first used in World War I. Their engines are more powerful and their weapons more destructive. But the basic goals of the fighter plane remain the same.

SOPWITH CAMEL
British—World War I

SPECIFICATIONS

ENGINE:
Number: 1
Manufacturer: Clerget (kler-JAY)
Model: 9 cylinder
Type: Air-cooled rotary
Rating: 130 horsepower

FIREPOWER:
2 Vickers .303-caliber machine guns

DIMENSIONS:
Wingspan: 28 feet
Length: 18 feet, 9 inches
Height: 8 feet, 6 inches

OTHER INFORMATION:
Manufacturer: Sopwith Aviation Company
Crew: 1
Maximum Takeoff Weight: 1,482 pounds
Ceiling: 21,000 feet
Maximum Range: 300 miles
Maximum Speed: 112 miles per hour

A total of 5,490 Sopwith Camels were built by the British for use in World War I. It was the most successful fighter plane of the war. Camel pilots brought down 1,294 enemy planes, more than any other fighter type!

One famous victim of a Sopwith Camel, Manfred von Richthofen of Germany, was known as the Red Baron. His Fokker Triplane (three-winged plane) is believed to have been shot down in 1918 by a Canadian Camel pilot named Roy Brown.

The airplane got its name because of the metal covering (cowling) on the back part (breeches) of the twin Vickers machine guns. The cowling gave the front of the plane a humped look, like a camel.

A pilot who sat in the open cockpit of the Sopwith Camel could feel the rush of the cold wind as he flew. Goggles helped protect his eyes, but the rotary engine threw oil into his face. He constantly wiped the goggles but couldn't help breathing in the fumes. He hoped he wouldn't get dizzy or sick.

Experienced and skillful pilots could outperform their German opponents in these small but speedy fighters. But for beginners, the Camel was difficult to fly. A tight turn could cause a spinout. A steep dive would make the plane tuck under and turn upside-down. Many pilots were killed in training!

Compared to today's aircraft the Sopwith Camel was a fragile craft. Its two wings were made of wood and fabric. The machine guns were mounted in front and only shot forward. To aim the fire you had to point the airplane directly at the target.

Camel pilots dove, twisted, turned, and shot at enemy aircraft. They attacked with the sun behind them so the enemy was blinded by the light! These dogfights took place high above the European countryside at speeds of over 100 miles per hour.

World War I pilots were responsible for a new word in aviation. Five "kills" and a pilot became a flying "ace." The term "ace" is still used today.

MITSUBISHI A6M ZERO

Japanese —World War II

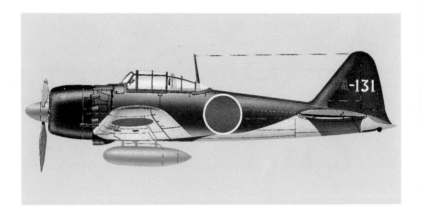

SPECIFICATIONS

ENGINE:
Number: 1
Manufacturer: Nakajima (nah-kah-JEE-mah)
Model: Sakae-21, 14 cylinder
Type: Piston
Rating: 1,130 horsepower

FIREPOWER:
2 7.7mm machine guns plus 2 Type-99 20mm cannons

DIMENSIONS:
Wingspan: 36 feet, 1 inch
Length: 29 feet, 11 inches
Height: 11 feet, 6 inches

OTHER INFORMATION:
Manufacturer: Mitsubishi
Crew: 1
Maximum Takeoff Weight: 6,025 pounds
Ceiling: 36,250 feet
Maximum Range: 1,479 miles
Maximum Speed: 339 miles per hour

On December 7, 1941, 353 warplanes took off from the decks of six Japanese aircraft carriers in the Pacific Ocean. Dive bombers, escorted by large numbers of A6M Zero fighter planes, surprised the United States Fleet at Pearl Harbor, Hawaii.

This Sunday morning attack killed 2,000 people and destroyed or disabled eight American battleships, three cruisers, and three destroyers. The Zeros played an important part in the raid. They sprayed ground targets with bullets as the dive bombers attacked the ships in the harbor. After Pearl Harbor the United States declared war on the Empire of Japan.

The A6M Zero was the best and most effective fighter plane in the early days of World War II. It was many months before America was able to produce a plane which matched its performance.

The A6M was nicknamed the Zero because the Japanese assigned it a number ending in zeroes. The Allies (mainly the U.S. and Britain) used first names to refer to enemy planes so the Zero is also sometimes called the "Zeke."

This lightweight, single-seat fighter ruled the sky above the Pacific, reaching speeds of over 300 miles per hour. The Zero could climb quickly and outmaneuver opposing airplanes. Its two machine guns and wing cannons packed a deadly punch to enemy aircraft!

The Zero had several major weaknesses, however. To keep the plane fast and agile the Japanese used no armor-plate protection around the pilot and the fuel tanks. The result was that the plane and pilot rarely could survive direct hits by American fighters such as the Wildcat and the Mustang.

Imagine the Zero pilot seated in his enclosed cockpit, as he waited to take off from the deck of a large carrier. He had no bulletproof windscreen. He knew that the three unprotected fuel tanks would likely explode in flames when hit by enemy fire. One of them was located just in front of the cockpit!

Many Zeros were used in the Kamikaze Corps late in the war. Young pilots deliberately crashed their planes directly into Allied ships on suicide missions. They did this for the honor of Japan and their Emperor.

The Kamikazes were responsible for sinking 36 American ships and damaging 1,000 others. But they couldn't stop the eventual defeat of Japan on September 2, 1945.

GRUMMAN F-4F WILDCAT
American—World War II

SPECIFICATIONS

ENGINE:
Number: 1
Manufacturer: Pratt and Whitney
Model: R-1830-86, 14 cylinder
Type: Piston
Rating: 1,200 horsepower

FIREPOWER:
6 .50-inch machine guns

DIMENSIONS:
Wingspan: 38 feet
Length: 28 feet, 11 inches
Height: 11 feet, 1 inch

OTHER INFORMATION:
Manufacturer: Grumman (GRUH-mun)
Crew: 1
Maximum Takeoff Weight: 7,952 pounds
Ceiling: 34,900 feet
Maximum Range: 850 miles
Maximum Speed: 318 miles per hour

The Grumman F-4F Wildcat was the Navy's first single-wing (monoplane) fighter. A short, thick body (fuselage) and folding wings made it an ideal plane for use on aircraft carriers.

In the early days of World War II, the Wildcat alone was responsible for holding off the Japanese in the Pacific. Although enemy Zeros could outclimb, outrun, and outmaneuver the small single-seat fighters, the Wildcats had the advantage in firepower and toughness. Six powerful .50-inch machine guns, four of them mounted on the wings, could tear apart a Zero's lightweight construction.

Wildcats were built with heavy armor plates around the pilot and self-sealing gas tanks. This rugged construction made the plane heavier and slower, but it was able to take a lot of punishment and still fly.

Pilots soon learned new combat tricks in dealing with the Zeros. Wildcats could dive faster than the Japanese planes, so they always tried to get an advantage by flying above the enemy.

Imagine a pilot seated in the cramped cockpit of the Wildcat as he scans the many dials and instruments. He looks below and sees a group of Zeros. His squadron leader gives the signal and the Wildcat dives through the Japanese formations. The pilot fires the machine guns, his finger never letting up on the trigger. Then the Wildcat quickly climbs again, before the enemy knows what hit them!

A pilot named John Thach was responsible for a maneuver called the "Thach Weave." Two Wildcats weaved in and out to protect each other's tails, thus cutting down on enemy hits.

Pilots became so skilled in combat that for every Wildcat lost, seven enemy aircraft were shot down! Navy ace Lieutenant Butch O'Hare shot down five Japanese bombers in one seven-minute attack. During this battle on February 20, 1942, the enemy lost 18 bombers while the Navy lost only two Wildcats!

Another flying ace, Marine Corps Captain Joseph Foss, shot down 27 Japanese planes in his Wildcat during World War II. He won the Congressional Medal of Honor for his efforts.

LOCKHEED P-38 LIGHTNING
American—World War II

SPECIFICATIONS

ENGINE:
Number: 2
Manufacturer: Allison
Model: V1710-89/91, 12 cylinder
Type: Piston
Rating: 1,425 horsepower each

FIREPOWER:
• 1 20mm cannon plus 4 .50-inch machine guns
     or
• A 3,200 bomb load
     or
• 10 5-inch rockets

DIMENSIONS:
Wingspan: 52 feet
Length: 37 feet, 10 inches
Height: 12 feet, 10 inches

OTHER INFORMATION:
Manufacturer: Lockheed
Crew: 1
Maximum Takeoff Weight: 20,700 pounds
Ceiling: 44,000 feet
Maximum Range: 1,175 miles
Maximum Speed: 414 miles per hour

The Lockheed P-38 Lightning was the only twin-engine American fighter built during World War II. Lightning pilots brought down more enemy aircraft in the Pacific than any other pilots. Major Richard Bong destroyed 40 enemy planes while flying his P-38. Another Lightning ace, Major Thomas McGuire, had 38 kills to his credit.

The P-38 had an outstanding record on the European front, too. German pilots called it "the fork-tailed devil"!

The Lightning was a unique-looking airplane: It had twin booms, which were two long sections that connected the tail to the wing and main body of the aircraft. It was also very large and heavy for a single-seat fighter plane. It weighed nearly as much as an Air Force bomber and its wingspan (52 feet) was much wider than that of other American fighters.

The Lightning was able to fly long distances, with a range of over 1,000 miles. On April 18, 1943, after the U.S. military broke secret Japanese radio codes, 16 P-38 fighters flew several hundred miles on a special mission. They intercepted and attacked the bomber carrying Japan's great naval hero, Admiral Yamamoto. The plane was shot down and Yamamoto was killed. It was a discouraging blow to the enemy and a warning from the Americans.

The P-38 was known for its speed and firepower. It was the world's first fighter to fly over 400 miles per hour in level flight. In September 1942 Lieutenant Colonel Cass Hough reached 780 miles per hour in his Lightning while in a 25,000-foot dive!

The P-38 had four .50-caliber machine guns plus one 20mm cannon mounted in its nose. It could blow enemy

aircraft out of the sky! Some models carried bombs or rockets. Others were used in photo-reconnaissance, to scout enemy territory and gather information. Instead of guns the plane carried three to five cameras.

The major weakness of the P-38 was that its size made it difficult to outmaneuver enemy fighters such as the German Messerschmitt. But it had many safety features. Armor plates were located in front, behind, and under the pilot's seat. Oxygen equipment was available in the cockpit and all fuel tanks were self-sealing and armor-plated. These features added to the pilot's confidence and performance during missions.

VOUGHT F-4U CORSAIR
American—World War II

SPECIFICATIONS

ENGINE:
Number: 1
Manufacturer: Pratt and Whitney
Model: R-2800-8W, 18 cylinder
Type: Piston
Rating: 2,250 horsepower

FIREPOWER:
• 6 .50-inch MG53-2 machine guns plus 2,000 pounds
  of bombs
          or
• 8 5-inch rockets

DIMENSIONS:
Wingspan: 40 feet, 11 inches
Length: 33 feet, 4 inches
Height: 15 feet, 1 inch

OTHER INFORMATION:
Manufacturer: Vought (VAHT)
Crew: 1
Maximum Takeoff Weight: 13,120 pounds
Ceiling: 37,000 feet
Maximum Range: 1,562 miles
Maximum Speed: 425 miles per hour

23

The Vought F-4U Corsair stayed in production longer than any other American fighter plane. The first model flew in May 1940 and the last one was built in February 1953. A total of 12,571 Corsairs were produced.

The F-4U was designed to be a carrier-based plane. It had a unique bent-wing design and a short landing gear. The outer wings folded up for storage on aircraft carrier decks.

The Corsair's Pratt and Whitney engine was the most powerful ever placed in a fighter. More than 2,000 horsepower made it capable of flying at speeds over 400 miles per hour with a full combat load.

Pilots found the Corsair difficult to land on carrier decks. Its landing speed was too high (90 miles per hour) and visibility was poor from the cockpit. As a result, the Corsairs were assigned to land-based squadrons. In 1944 the war in the Pacific made it necessary to reassign some of them back to aircraft carriers.

Pilots adapted themselves to the Corsairs and these rugged and reliable planes proved themselves to be excellent fighters. They had speed, maneuverability, and firepower. The six .50-caliber machine guns mounted in the outer wings could handle any enemy fighter. And they could easily carry a huge load of bombs. During one mission, the Corsair was used as a dive bomber and carried 4,000 pounds of bombs!

Corsairs flew 64,051 missions (9,581 from carriers) during World War II. A total of 2,140 enemy aircraft were shot down with a loss of 189 F-4Us. That's 11 enemy planes

downed for every Corsair lost! It's no wonder the Japanese called them "Whistling Death"!

Corsair aces during the war included Colonel Gregory "Pappy" Boyington, with 28 kills, and Lieutenant Robert M. Hansen, with 25.

The F-4U remained in service with the U.S. Navy until the mid-1950s. It was used by the French Navy until the early 1960s. The Corsair was the last piston engine fighter plane to be produced by the United States.

NORTH AMERICAN
P-51 MUSTANG
American —World War II

SPECIFICATIONS

ENGINE:
Number: 1
Manufacturer: Packard
Model: Rolls Royce "Merlin" V-1650-3, 12 cylinder
Type: Piston
Rating: 1,430 horsepower

FIREPOWER:
- 6 .50-inch MG53-2 machine guns plus 2,000 pounds
  of bombs
       or
- 6 5-inch rockets

DIMENSIONS:
Wingspan: 37 feet, ¼ inch
Length: 32 feet, 3 inches
Height: 13 feet, 8 inches

OTHER INFORMATION:
Manufacturer: North American Aviation
Crew: 1
Maximum Takeoff Weight: 12,100 pounds
Ceiling: 41,900 feet
Maximum Range: 2,080 miles
Maximum Speed: 437 miles per hour

The P-51 Mustang was one of the best all-around single-seat fighter planes of World War II. It was first built for British Royal Air Force pilots, who used the Mustang for low-altitude missions. The RAF would fly over enemy trains, troops, and other targets, spraying them with heavy machine-gun fire (strafing).

But the Americans needed a long-range, high-altitude fighter that could escort heavy bombers on daylight raids into Germany. When the P-51's original Allison engine was replaced with the more powerful Rolls-Royce Merlin engine, the Mustang's performance soared. Its speed rose to about 440 miles an hour. Its range increased when it was fitted with two additional 110-gallon wing fuel tanks. The Air Force knew it had found the plane it needed to escort American bombers deep into the heart of enemy territory.

In January 1944 the Mustang became the first U.S. fighter plane to cross the German border. A few months later Mustangs began escorting squadrons of B-17 and B-24 bombers. One high-ranking Nazi said that the day he saw American fighters over Berlin was the day he knew Germany would lose the war. Those fighters he saw were P-51 Mustangs!

The Mustang pilot sat in a cockpit in which every available space was crammed with a gauge, handle, or switch. Even the cockpit floor was filled with instruments. Some flyers said, "You don't climb into a '51, you pull it on like a pair of pants."

The Mustang pilot was always on the lookout for enemy planes. His job was to protect the bombers while they dropped their payloads on enemy targets, then get them home safely.

Suddenly there were German fighters at 3 o'clock! A group of Messerschmitt 109s were preparing to attack and blast the bombers out of the sky. But the Mustang had something to say about that!

The speedy little fighter was sensitive to the lightest touch of the controls. A push of the stick and it went into a 500-mile-per-hour dive. It climbed and looped, twisted and turned, above and behind the enemy planes. The Mustang outmaneuvered the best of the enemy's fighters.

The pilot used the heavy gunsight behind the thick windshield in the cockpit to get the Messerschmitt in his sights. When his finger pushed the trigger switch, all six .50-caliber machine guns fired at the same time with deadly power. The pilot recorded a direct hit!

For every P-51 lost in combat in the war, seven enemy planes were downed! Mustang pilots shot down more aircraft than any other American fighter on the European front.

MESSERSCHMITT ME 262-A STURMVOGEL

German—World War II

SPECIFICATIONS

ENGINE:
Number: 2
Manufacturer: Junkers
Model: Jumo 004B-1j
Type: Turbojet
Rating: 1,984 pounds of thrust each

FIREPOWER:
4 30mm MK-108 cannons

DIMENSIONS:
Wingspan: 40 feet, 11½ inches
Length: 34 feet, 11 inches
Height: 12 feet, 8 inches

OTHER INFORMATION:
Manufacturer: Messerschmitt (MES-ser-shmit)
Crew: 1
Maximum Takeoff Weight: 14,101 pounds
Ceiling: 32,565 feet
Maximum Range: 652 miles
Maximum Speed: 541 miles per hour

The Messerschmitt ME 262-A Sturmvogel ("stormbird" in German) was the first operational jet fighter in the world. This German plane was powered by two turbojet engines, each with a thrust (forward force) of 1,984 pounds. The result was a single-seat fighter plane which could fly at a speed of 541 miles per hour.

The Sturmvogel was faster than the Allied fighters. It could outclimb, outrun, and outdive the best of them. The Allies became alarmed and increased their bombing raids against enemy jet airfields. But there was no reason for fear. The Germans introduced the plane too late in World War II to have an impact on the outcome.

The Sturmvogel could have been brought into the fighting in 1943 instead of late 1944. But Adolph Hitler, the dictator of Germany, insisted it be used as a bomber instead of as a fighter, which was its original role. This proved to be a costly mistake for the enemy but a lucky break for the Allies. By the time the Messerschmitt became operational as a fighter, the German fuel reserves were shrinking and the poorly trained pilots couldn't use their superior speed to their advantage. Only one quarter of the 1,433 turbojets produced by Messerschmitt were used in the war.

Many Sturmvogels were destroyed in combat and outmaneuvered by the slower American and British piston-engined aircraft. Despite their slower planes, the Allied pilots were more experienced in high-altitude dogfights.

The Sturmvogel had plenty of firepower. It was armed with four fixed 30mm short-barreled cannons mounted in its steel nose cone. It could also carry two 550-pound bombs.

Britain introduced its own jet fighter, called the Gloster Meteor, late in the war. It had two turbojets like the ME262-A but was about 100 miles per hour slower.

LOCKHEED F-80 SHOOTING STAR
American—Korean War, 1950s

SPECIFICATIONS

ENGINE:
Number: 1
Manufacturer: Allison
Model: J-33-A-23
Type: Turbojet
Rating: 4,000 pounds of thrust

FIREPOWER:
- 6 .50-inch machine guns plus eight rockets
    or
- 2,000 pounds of bombs

DIMENSIONS:
Wingspan: 39 feet, 10 inches
Length: 34 feet, 6½ inches
Height: 11 feet, 8 inches

OTHER INFORMATION:
Manufacturer: Lockheed
Crew: 1
Maximum Takeoff Weight: 14,500 pounds
Ceiling: 45,000 feet
Maximum Range: 1,100 miles
Maximum Speed: 580 miles per hour

The Lockheed P-80 Shooting Star was the first American fighter with a jet engine. It flew in January 1944 but the war ended before it was ever used in combat.

Aircraft in World War II had mainly piston engines and were propeller-driven. They couldn't go faster than 425–450 miles per hour. The use of jet engines in airplanes opened up the possibility of speeds and altitudes never before reached in aviation.

After the war, the P-80's "P" for pursuit was changed to "F" for fighter by the Air Force. The F-80 continued to be built by Lockheed and in 1947 it set a speed record of 623.8 miles per hour in a dive.

On June 25, 1950, North Korea, armed with Russian equipment, invaded South Korea. A United Nations force, made up mainly of United States troops and supplies, came to South Korea's aid. They drove back the enemy, advancing deep into North Korean territory. Communist China entered the war on North Korea's side and used Russian MiG-15 jet fighters against American aircraft.

The F-80 battled the MiGs in the skies above Korea. The straight-winged American plane could fly level at a speed of 580 miles per hour, but that was 80 miles per hour slower than the speedy Russian fighter. Many American pilots were World War II veterans and their combat experience made up for the differences in speed.

On November 8, 1950, Lieutenant Russell Brown, flying an F-80 Shooting Star, brought down a MiG-15 fighter. It was the world's first all-jet dogfight! However, the Shooting Star was no match for the swept-wing MiG. It was soon replaced in Korea by the F-86 Sabre jet.

A two-seat version of the F-80 (called the T-33) was used to train jet pilots for many years. The instructor sat in the back seat and the plane was equipped with only two machine guns.

The F-80 stayed in production for 15 years, until August 1959. Different models were built for a variety of tasks. Some were used for photo-reconnaissance. Instead of the six .50-inch machine guns in the lower portion of the nose, the airplane carried five cameras to take pictures.

NORTH AMERICAN F-86 SABRE
American—Korean War, 1950s–1960s

SPECIFICATIONS

ENGINE:
Number: 1
Manufacturer: General Electric
Model: J-47-GE-27
Type: Turbojet
Rating: 8,920 pounds of thrust

FIREPOWER:
• 6 .50-inch machine guns
            or
• 16 5-inch rockets

DIMENSIONS:
Wingspan: 39 feet, 1 inch
Length: 38 feet, 10 inches
Height: 14 feet, 8¾ inches

OTHER INFORMATION:
Manufacturer: North American
Crew: 1
Maximum Takeoff Weight: 15,680 pounds
Ceiling: 49,000 feet
Maximum Range: 1,200 miles
Maximum Speed: More than 650 miles per hour

The North American F-86 Sabre is considered one of the best combat aircraft of all time. The F-86 was the first American fighter to be designed with swept-back wings and tail. A powerful General Electric turbojet engine helped the Sabre set a world speed record of 715.69 miles per hour in 1953.

It was the Sabre that the Air Force depended upon to do battle with the Russian MiG-15s in the Korean War (1950–1953). The MiGs could fly several thousand feet higher than the Sabres and they had an edge in fire-power, being armed with two to four large cannons. They also outnumbered the American planes two-to-one and their lighter weight allowed them to climb faster in combat. But their top speed was slightly slower than the Sabre and the MiG pilots were inexperienced fighters, while most Sabre pilots were World War II veterans, experienced and well-trained in fighting tactics. Dogfights in the Korean War took place more than 40,000 feet above the ground at speeds over 650 miles per hour!

Imagine a typical pilot as he sat in his pressurized cockpit streaking across the sky. He flew one of four F-86 Sabres in formation and watched closely for enemy fighters. He soon entered "MiG Alley," an area of North Korean territory where most air combat took place.

The pilot spotted three enemy MiGs a few thousand feet below the Sabres. Signaling the others, the four planes split into groups of two. One pair dove toward the enemy at high speed.

The pilot used his radar range gunsight and fired his six heavy machine guns. The Sabre's guns had a higher rate of fire than the MiG cannons. This increased the chances of hitting the fast-moving Russian plane.

The enemy broke to the left and dove quickly to get away from the deadly fire. One MiG climbed rapidly only to be met by the second pair of Sabres at the higher altitude. Working as a team, the Sabre jets scored direct hits on all three enemy aircraft with no losses of their own.

By the time the Korean War ended on July 27, 1953, F-86 jets had shot down 827 MiG-15s. Only 78 Sabres were lost. For every one Sabre brought down, more than 10 enemy planes were destroyed. It's no wonder the F-86 Sabre was known as the "MiG Killer"!

But the real winners in the skies over Korea were the American pilots, whose skill, experience, and training were far better than their opponents. All 39 jet aces in Korea flew F-86 Sabres. Together, they shot down 305 MiGs!

LOCKHEED F-104 STARFIGHTER
American—Late 1950s–1970s

SPECIFICATIONS

ENGINE:
Number: 1
Manufacturer: General Electric
Model: J-79-GE-3A
Type: Turbojet
Rating: 15,000 pounds of thrust

FIREPOWER:
1 Vulcan 20mm revolving cannon and 1 Sidewinder missile on each wing tip

DIMENSIONS:
Wingspan: 21 feet, 11 inches
Length: 54 feet, 9 inches
Height: 13 feet, 6 inches

OTHER INFORMATION:
Manufacturer: Lockheed
Crew: 1
Maximum Takeoff Weight: 22,000 pounds
Ceiling: 55,000 feet
Maximum Range: 2,200 miles
Maximum Speed: More than 1,400 miles per hour

The Lockheed F-104 Starfighter was the first jet ever built to fly more than twice the speed of sound. First introduced in 1958, it shot across the sky at better than 1,400 miles per hour!

Supersonic aircraft are those which fly faster than the speed of sound. Above 40,000 feet, sound travels at 660 miles per hour, called Mach 1. Mach 2, twice the speed of sound, is 1,320 miles per hour.

The Starfighter was one of the most unusual-looking fighter planes ever produced. It was once described as a "missile with a man in it." It had a dagger shape and a very long pointed nose. The wings were very short and straight and placed far back on the body of the airplane. Each of the wing panels measured only seven and a half feet. The edges were so razor sharp that protective covers were used to prevent the ground crew from being injured!

The pilot of a supersonic jet fighter like the F-104 sat in a pressurized and air-conditioned cockpit. In case of an emergency, he escaped by blowing the hatch and ejecting from the plane. Still seated, the pilot hurtled through the air. Then the seat belt unsnapped, freeing him automatically, and a parachute opened at a pre-set altitude.

The Starfighter is the only airplane to hold world records in three categories at the same time. It set a speed record of 1,404.19 miles per hour in 1958, and an altitude mark of 103,389 feet in 1959.

The F-104 also set a rate-of-climb record in 1958. It streaked to 82,020 feet (more than 15 miles up) in 4 minutes and 26 seconds. Almost 20 years later, in 1977, it established a low-altitude speed record of 988.26 miles per hour.

The Starfighter was the first fighter to be armed with the Vulcan 20mm revolving cannon. A rotating group of barrels was able to fire over 1,000 rounds of ammunition in 15-second bursts. This awesome amount of firepower was ideal for ground-strafing and attack missions. For air combat, the F-104 carried a Sidewinder missile in each wing tip.

The Starfighter wasn't widely used in the United States. But different versions were produced by Lockheed and then manufactured in countries such as Germany, the Netherlands, Belgium, Italy, and Canada. Many models are still used today in air forces around the world.

HAWKER SIDDELEY HARRIER MK-1
British —1970s —1980s

SPECIFICATIONS

ENGINE:
Number: 1
Manufacturer: Rolls Royce
Model: Bristol Pegasus Mk 101
Type: Turbofan
Rating: 19,000 pounds of thrust

FIREPOWER:
5,000 pounds of a variety of guns, bombs, and rockets

DIMENSIONS:
Wingspan: 25 feet, 3 inches
Length: 45 feet, 6 inches
Height: 11 feet, 4 inches

OTHER INFORMATION:
Manufacturer: Hawker Siddeley (HAH-ker SID-lee)
Crew: 1
Maximum Takeoff Weight: 25,000 pounds
Ceiling: 50,000 feet
Maximum Range: 2,300 miles
Maximum Speed: More than 737 miles per hour

47

The Hawker Siddeley Harrier MK-1 was the first Vertical/ Short Takeoff and Landing (V/STOL) fighter in the world. Other airplanes need a runway or airfield to take off and land. The British-built Harrier takes off straight up in the air. It can be used in forest or jungle clearings, or on beaches, roads, and the decks of ships at sea.

The Harrier uses the Pegasus turbofan engine with four attached rotating exhaust nozzles. The exhaust nozzles are aimed down on takeoff and the Harrier rises up and off the ground. As the aircraft goes up, the pilot turns the nozzles slowly to the side to get forward movement as well as lift. Once a certain speed is reached, the nozzles are turned completely to the rear. Then the engine's thrust is used to push the jet forward like any other airplane. Landings are the reverse of takeoffs.

If a short forward run is possible, the Harrier can take off with a heavier weapon load. Weapons are carried under the wings and fuselage. A typical combat load might include a pair of 30mm guns, two 1,000-pound bombs, and an assortment of rockets.

Different versions of the Harrier are used by the United States Marines, the British Royal Air Force, the Spanish Navy, and the Indian Navy. There are one- and two-seat models. Those used mainly for reconnaissance carry cameras instead of weapons.

A Sea Harrier V/STOL fighter was first flown from an aircraft carrier in the late 1970s. An on-deck ski-jump type of launching ramp allowed this Harrier to take off at a lower speed. This saved fuel and permitted heavier loads to be carried than from a flat deck takeoff.

Sea Harriers were used by the British in the Battle of the Falkland Islands in May 1982. Argentina claimed that the islands belonged to them, even though a colony of British citizens lived there. British forces successfully engaged in combat against Argentina to prevent a takeover. A total of 28 Sea Harriers flew 2,380 missions. They destroyed 27 enemy aircraft in air-to-air combat with no losses of their own.

In 1971, a Harrier set a new international time-to-height record for jet aircraft. It reached 29,528 feet in one minute 44.7 seconds and 39,370 feet in two minutes 22.7 seconds.

MCDONNELL DOUGLAS F-4E
PHANTOM II

American—Vietnam War, Late 1960s–1980s

SPECIFICATIONS

ENGINE:
Number: 2
Manufacturer: General Electric
Model: J79-GE-17
Type: Turbojet with afterburner
Rating: 17,900 pounds of thrust each

FIREPOWER:
1 M61 20mm multibarrel cannon and a 16,000-pound load of bombs, missiles, and rockets

DIMENSIONS:
Wingspan: 38 feet, 5 inches
Length: 62 feet, 11¾ inches
Height: 16 feet, 5½ inches

OTHER INFORMATION:
Manufacturer: McDonnell Douglas
Crew: 2
Maximum Takeoff Weight: 59,000 pounds
Ceiling: 70,000 feet
Maximum Range: 2,300 miles
Maximum Speed: More than 1,584 miles per hour

The McDonnell Douglas F-4E Phantom II was one of the most outstanding fighter planes ever built. It had power, speed, and maneuverability. It could be used in air combat, ground attack, and reconnaissance missions. The F-4E operated from the decks of aircraft carriers and was the first fighter capable of fully automatic carrier landings.

The F-4E model was first built in the late 1960s. It was often called "the fastest gun in the sky." A powerful Vulcan 20mm cannon fired at a rate of 100 rounds of ammunition per second. That's an incredible 6,000 rounds per minute!

The cannon was housed in the forward fuselage underbelly of the airplane. That left the wing and lower fuselage areas free to carry other weapons. The F-4E carried a combat load of 16,000 pounds of bombs, missiles, and rockets. It was usually a mixture of infrared (heat-seeking) and radar-guided weapons.

The F-4E saw heavy action in the Vietnam War in the late 1960s and early 1970s. The United States supported the South Vietnamese in their conflict against Communist-backed North Vietnam. The war was fought in the jungles of Southeast Asia. Phantom jets fought against Russian-built MiGs high in the skies above Vietnam.

The F-4Es were better equipped and armed than the enemy. Phantom pilots used their advanced radar tracking and automatic weapon-launching systems to destroy enemy planes over great distances. The Phantom's radar could detect a MiG more than 30 miles away and its weapons could seek out and destroy the enemy up to 12 miles away.

Since the first model F-4A Phantom flew in 1958, over a dozen new speed, altitude, and time-to-height records have been set. Many versions have been built and used in the air forces of countries throughout the world. In addition to the United States Air Force, Navy, and Marines, the F-4E has seen service in Germany, Greece, Iran, Israel, Japan, South Korea, Spain, Turkey, and Great Britain, and the Israelis have successfully flown Phantom jets in combat in the Middle East. F-4 Phantom jets have been produced in larger numbers than any other Western supersonic fighter.

MIKOYAN MiG-25 FOXBAT
Russian—Late 1960s–1980s and beyond

SPECIFICATIONS

ENGINE:
Number: 2
Manufacturer: Tumansky (too-MAHN-skee)
Model: R-266
Type: Turbojet with afterburner
Rating: 24,250 pounds of thrust each

FIREPOWER:
4 air-to-air missiles on underwing attachments

DIMENSIONS:
Wingspan: 45 feet, 9 inches
Length: 78 feet, 1¾ inches
Height: 20 feet, ¼ inch

OTHER INFORMATION:
Manufacturer: Mikoyan (mi-kah-YAHN)
Crew: 1
Maximum Takeoff Weight: 77,150 pounds
Ceiling: 80,000 feet
Maximum Range: More than 1,400 miles
Maximum Speed: More than 1,850 miles per hour

The Mikoyan MiG-25 Foxbat is the fastest fighter plane in the world today. This Russian-built aircraft is powered by two Tumansky turbojet engines with afterburners. It is capable of speeds nearly three times the speed of sound (Mach 3).

In 1967 the Foxbat set a speed record in level flight of 1,852.61 miles per hour. In 1977 a MiG-25 set an absolute height record of 123,524 feet.

The Foxbat has swept-back wings and twin tail fins. The airframe is made mainly of steel, with titanium in places that would be subjected to extreme heat. Although the MiG can fly at high speeds, it has difficulty maintaining them.

There are half as many cockpit instruments in the MiG-25 as in the F-4E Phantom jet. The weapon sight is smaller and the launching system isn't as advanced. The Foxbat carries four air-to-air missiles on its underwing attachments.

The MiG-25 computer operates along with a ground-based flight control system. It allows the plane to be directed to its target over long ranges.

Although the Foxbat can reach speeds of Mach 3 at altitudes over 80,000 feet, this is not so useful in combat; it would be likely to engage in combat at lower speeds and altitudes. Once the advantage of speed is taken away, the Foxbat comes up short in maneuverability and endurance. For this reason, it's been used mainly in a reconnaissance role. The reconnaissance version of the

MiG-25 carries no weapons. Instead, it has five camera windows and advanced radar and navigation systems.

Israel witnessed the Foxbat's reconnaissance capabilities in 1971 and early 1972, when four Foxbats flew out of Egypt and carried out high-speed reconnaissance missions off the Israeli coast and down the Sinai Peninsula. Israeli Phantom jets were unable to make contact with the speedy MiGs.

In addition to the USSR, Syria, Algeria, Libya, and India all use MiG-25 aircraft in their forces.

GENERAL DYNAMICS F-16
FIGHTING FALCON
American—1980s and beyond

SPECIFICATIONS

ENGINE:
Number: 1
Manufacturer: Pratt and Whitney
Model: F100-PW-200
Type: Turbofan with afterburner
Rating: 25,000 pounds of thrust

FIREPOWER:
1 rapid-fire 20mm multibarrel cannon and 2 infrared
heat-seeking missiles on wing tips

DIMENSIONS:
Wingspan: 32 feet, 10 inches
Length: 49 feet, 6 inches
Height: 16 feet, 8½ inches

OTHER INFORMATION:
Manufacturer: General Dynamics
Crew: 1
Maximum Takeoff Weight: 35,400 pounds
Ceiling: Over 50,000 feet
Maximum Range: More than 2,415 miles
Maximum Speed: More than 1,320 miles per hour

The General Dynamics F-16 Fighting Falcon was the jet fighter picked by the U.S. Air Force to replace its F-4 Phantom IIs. Fifteen other countries have followed suit and now use F-16s in their armed forces. First combat use of the Fighting Falcon was by the Israeli Air Force. They used eight aircraft to successfully destroy Iraq's Osirak nuclear reactor on June 7, 1981.

The world-wide success of this supersonic jet fighter is due to its overall performance, speed, maneuverability, and modern equipment. The Fighting Falcon is a lightweight, speedy fighter powered by a Pratt and Whitney turbofan engine. Its 25,000 pounds of thrust and its afterburner, which burns extra fuel for additional thrust, allow it to reach speeds of more than 1,320 miles per hour, twice the speed of sound (Mach 2).

Built to match the ability of the Russian MiG, the F-16 is armed with a Vulcan rapid-fire 20mm multibarrel cannon. It has a General Electric ammunition handling system and gunsight.

The gunsight is part of the HUD (Head-Up-Display) mounted in front of the pilot's face in the cockpit. The HUD allows the pilot to see important information immediately without turning away. All radar, navigation, and tracking information also appears on HUD.

The F-16 carries two infrared heat-seeking missiles, one on each wing tip. The Fighting Falcon is capable of air-to-air combat with gun and missiles and air-to-ground attack with gun, rockets, bombs, and other weapons which can be stored under the fuselage and under the wings.

At supersonic speeds the high force of gravity (g-force) pushes the pilot back in his seat. For his comfort, the seat in the air-conditioned cockpit of the F-16 slopes back and the rudder pedals are raised. A transparent bubble canopy provides the pilot with a clear all-around view.

The flight control system consists of an onboard computer which senses unsteadiness in the aircraft. The system automatically makes adjustments.

Future plans for the Fighting Falcon include even more advanced cockpit displays and controls and improved radar- and weapon-launching systems. F-16 developments by the Air Force are planned well into the next century!

GLOSSARY

Ace—An expert in combat flying who has brought down at least five enemy aircraft.

Afterburner—A device attached to the tailpipe of the engine which uses hot exhaust gases to burn extra fuel for more thrust.

Armor—A protective covering such as metal plates on fighter planes.

Boom—A projecting beam on an airplane which connects the tail surfaces to the main body.

Breech—The thick, back part of a firearm.

Caliber—The diameter of a bullet; the inside diameter of the gun barrel.

Canopy—The covering over the cockpit of an airplane.

Ceiling—The maximum altitude that a fighter plane should reach in combat.

Cowling—A metal covering.

Dogfight—Combat between fighter planes at close range.

Fuselage (FEW-suh-lahj)—The main body of an airplane.

G-force—The pull or force of gravity which increases in an aircraft as its speed increases.

Horsepower—A unit for measuring the power of an engine.

HUD—Head-Up-Display mounted in front of the pilot's face in the cockpit; all radar, navigation, and tracking information appear on HUD.

Infrared—Heat-seeking weapons (missiles) which lock on to and follow the heat rays coming from the exhaust of enemy aircraft.

Kamikazes (kah-mi-KAH-zees)—Japanese pilots of World War II who flew suicide missions by crashing their airplanes full of weapons into an enemy ship.

Mach 1—The speed of sound; 660 miles per hour at 40,000 feet.

Maneuverability (mah-new-ver-ah-BIL-i-tee)—The ability to perform skillful movements.

Monoplane—An airplane with one wing.

Nuclear reactor—A plant which produces atomic energy in controlled surroundings.

Payload—The bomb load of an aircraft.

Piston engine—An engine powered by pistons; pistons are solid metal pieces in the cylinder moved by a rod which is connected to the crankshaft; the movement of the pistons is sent on to the crankshaft.

Pressurized—To keep a normal atmospheric pressure inside an airplane at high altitudes so the pilot can breathe properly.

Propeller—Rotating shaft fitted with angled blades which provides thrust in air and propels an airplane forward.

Reconnaissance (ree-KAH-na-sans)—The act of obtaining information about an enemy area; a survey or examination.

Rotary engine—An early-model engine in which the cylinders and crankcase rotated around a crank.

Rudder—The flat, movable pieces of metal attached vertically to the back of the plane, used to steer the plane.

Strafe—To attack with machine-gun fire from low-flying aircraft.

Supersonic—Faster than the speed of sound.

Thach Weave (THACH WEEV)—A maneuver developed during World War II, in which two F-4F Wildcats weaved in and out to protect each other's tails, cutting down on enemy hits.

Titanium (ty-TAY-nee-um)—A hard, gray metal which resists corrosion (being worn or rusted away).

Triplane (TRY-playn)—An airplane with three wings placed one above the other.

Turbine (TER-byn)—An engine driven by the pressure of steam, water, or air against the curved vanes of a wheel or set of wheels.

Turbofan—A fan driven by a turbine in a ducted fan jet engine.

Turbojet—A jet engine in which the energy of the jet operates a turbine, which in turn operates an air compressor.

V/STOL—Vertical/Short Take-Off and Landing; an aircraft which takes off and lands straight up or down or on a short runway.